# Contents

## Inside-Out

Inside I play peaceful games in my chair . . .

outside I hunt for the dragon's lair.

Inside is for quiet girls and boys . . .

outside is the place for a lot of noise!

Sometimes, inside, I run and shout . . .

and Mum says I'm getting things inside-out!

# In Our House

There's a quiet mouse in the kitchen,
and a black spider under the stairs,
my Mum says there are animals everywhere;
there's a gentle moth that dances
all round the bathroom light,
and ants come in from the garden at night;
outside my window some swallows have a nest,
but . . . a teddy comes to bed with me
and he's the best.

TOYS

## On Safari

I'm on safari in the park,
there are lions and tigers about.
I creep along slowly, close to the ground,
if I see one I'll give Dad a shout.
I'll watch out for any movement
as I crawl from tree to tree;
I know that lions and tigers
could make mincemeat out of me!

## Grandmother's Box

There was a smart red soldier who marched on the floor
and a green glass marble that rolled under the door;
a black shoelace snake and a piece of white string,
a small, pink ballerina who danced on a swing;

an old brown rabbit with torn, purple hands
and a twisted shell full of soft, yellow sand;
but we did not find the pair of blue socks
that Grandmother was sure she had put in her box.

## The Summer Fete

We rode ponies at the summer fete
and ran in a three legged race.

My brother won the fancy dress –
you should have seen his face!

There were prizes for the treasure hunt
and a game called Pick a Straw.
Mum drank tea in a huge marquee
while we slipped off to explore.

I reached down deep in the lucky dip
and pulled out a little toy cat.
My brother said, 'Wow! Do you see what I see?
I'm having a ride on that!'

So we had three goes on a tiny train
till Mum came looking for us,

and even though we'd had a great time
we both made a terrible fuss . . .

all the way home.

## When The Thunder Roars

When the thunder roars it starts to rain,
splashing long, wet streaks on the window pane;
our dog hides her head under black and white paws
and my cat climbs the curtains with long, sharp claws;
Dad says the clouds are banging together,
the noise always wakes my new baby brother;
I sit on Mum's knee, near the door,
waiting for a flash and another thunder roar.

# Bouncy Castle

We bounced on the bouncy castle
and I jumped really high.
My sister stayed close to the edge
where Mum could keep an eye.
'Now just be careful,' Mum said,
as I bounced up high again,
and that was when the tip of my chin
met the knee of my best friend Ben!

## Barbeques

I love to see chops and sausages
sizzling on the grid,
and a pot of barbeque sauce that smells
so good when I lift the lid.

I love barbeques in our garden
when the weather is really hot,
and if Mum and Dad look the other way,
I'm ready to scoff the lot!